Midnight

MARK GREENWOOD
illustrated by FRANÉ LESSAC

CANDLEWICK PRESS

A FOAL IS BORN AT MIDNIGHT, ON A CATTLE RANCH
IN AUSTRALIA.

Coal black.
Star ablaze.
Moonlight in her eyes.

Guy handles Midnight as a foal.
He trains her as a filly.

They muster cattle in the high country.
Trust bonds horse and rider.

But in the winter of 1914,
the drums of a distant war are beating.
Guy and Midnight heed the nation's call.

The wind blows in Midnight's mane.

And they ride to join the cavalry.

Back straight,
head high,
at the farewell parade.

Proud rider,
bound for battle,
holds his black mare's reins.

The fleet steams across windswept seas.
But word passes down the line.
"We've been ordered to the Turkish coast," says Guy.
"Horses stay behind."

At the first port of call, Midnight is unloaded.

Guy sails on alone.

Front lines.
Gallipoli.
Sniper. Mortar.
Pelting rain. Biting frost.
The soldiers retreat,
feet frozen in slush.

After four months in the trenches, Guy boards a ship bound for Cairo. He hopes to find the horse he left behind.

In the shadow of the pyramids,
Guy searches the lines,
calling Midnight's name.
He wonders if he'll ever see
his beloved mare again.

He finds Midnight after drills,
when the troops let off steam—
wrestling on horseback, racing their steeds.
"Did you think I'd forget you?" Guy whispers.

Midnight whinnies and tosses her head.

Horse and rider, reunited, patrol the dunes of Sinai.

Weeks in the saddle.

Water is scarce.

Shrapnel kicks up dust.

Bullets clip Guy's hat.

In battle, Midnight works hard for her praise.

Weary riders dismount on the outskirts of an ancient city. *Beersheba*.
The enemy entrenched there defends seven wells of water,
more precious than gold.

Hours quiver by.

Guy rests in Midnight's shade, chewing on beef and biscuit.
He uncorks his canteen.

Midnight paws the sand.

Guy lays his head on her
shoulder and shares a secret
between horse and rider.

It is the hour before darkness. Squadron leaders saddle up.
A shiver gallops down Guy's back.
A stirring of men.
A jostle of horses and buckling straps.

Midnight's ears flick forward
to attention. She trots into formation,
pounding her hooves.

"Forwaaard!"

The canter quickens to a charge.
Midnight spurs to full gallop.
The earth drums beneath her.

Guy crouches in the saddle. Bullets zip past.
Riders tumble.
Horses fall.

Midnight arches her back and hurdles the enemy trench.
Guy braces for the bullet.
It passes through Midnight
and lodges beside Guy's spine.

Night falls.
Stretcher-bearers load casualties onto carts.
Guy waits his turn.

He cries and lets go of Midnight's reins,
beloved mare beside him.

Coal black.
Star ablaze.
Moonlight in her eyes.

Author's Note

Midnight is inspired by the folklore of the Haydon family, who have bred magnificent horses, including Midnight, at their ranch in New South Wales, Australia, since the early 1830s.

Midnight was born on October 31, 1905, beside the crystal waters of the Pages River in Blandford. She was coal black with a single snow-white star on her forehead. Midnight was highly prized for the gentle strength of Moonlight, her mother, and the speed of her father, an outstanding stallion, unbeaten at the quarter-mile sprint.

Guy Haydon, 12th Light Horse Regiment, B Squadron, astride Midnight

Guy and Midnight in the desert

Guy Haydon, army portrait

The Charge at Beersheba

On October 31, 1917, beneath the copper glow of the fading sun, the 4th and 12th Australian Light Horse Regiments took part in one of the last great cavalry charges in history. Three thousand well-entrenched Turkish soldiers stood between eight hundred mounted soldiers and the ancient wells of Beersheba. The successful charge led to the capture of Jerusalem and the subsequent collapse of the Ottoman Empire.

Lieutenant Haydon survived the charge, but a bullet lodged in his back, just missing his spine. He was taken to the Australian General Hospital in Cairo, where the bullet was removed. Guy sent it to his mother, wrapped in a letter describing the famous charge. The bullet and letter are kept at the Haydon ranch, where Midnight was born.

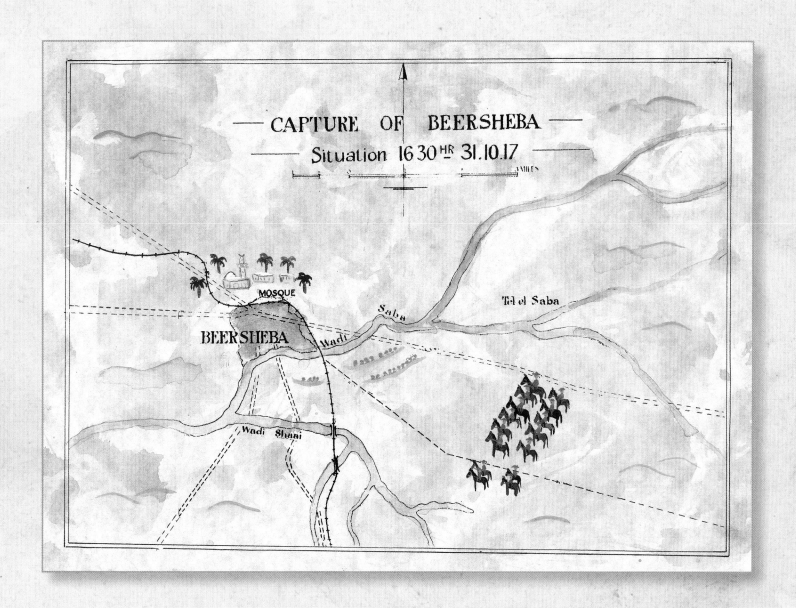

*Dedicated to the Light Horsemen
and their horses*

First U.S. edition 2015

Library of Congress Catalog Card Number 2013957478
ISBN 978-0-7636-7466-3

CCP 20 19 18 17 16 15
10 9 8 7 6 5 4 3 2 1

Printed in Shenzhen, Guangdong, China

This book was typeset in Mrs. Eaves.
The illustrations were created in gouache.

Candlewick Press
99 Dover Street
Somerville, Massachusetts 02144

visit us at www.candlewick.com

ACKNOWLEDGMENTS

Special thanks to Peter and Ali Haydon for inviting
us to Midnight's home and allowing us to view
Guy Haydon's letters from the trenches at Gallipoli
and the Middle East, along with other personal
family archives.

Thanks also to Frank and Lyne Greenwood,
Sarah Foster, Sue Whiting, Gayna Murphy, Robert
Stuart Hay, Karen Bell, Evangeline Read, Kelvin
Combie, Millie and Ann Singer, and Arynn Regan.
Our gratitude to Gil Asman and family for hospitality
while we researched in Be'er Sheva (Beersheba).

SOURCES

BOOKS

Crombie, Kelvin. *Journey to Beersheba.* Mundaring, West
   Australia: Heritage Resources, 2011.
Daley, Paul. *Beersheba: A Journey Through Australia's Forgotten
   War.* Melbourne: Melbourne University Press, 2009.
Davison, F. D. *The Wells of Beersheba.* North Ryde, New
   South Wales: Angus & Robertson, 1985.
Hamilton, Jill. *First to Damascus.* Kenthurst, New South
   Wales: Kangaroo Press, 2002.
Hill, Anthony. *Animal Heroes.* Melbourne: Penguin
   Australia, 2005.
Hollis, Kenneth. *Thunder of the Hooves.* Loftus, New South
   Wales: Australian Military History Publications, 2008.
Idriess, Ion L. *The Desert Column.* Sydney: Angus &
   Robertson, 1932.
Jones, Ian. *The Australian Light Horse.* Sydney: Time-Life
   Australia, 1987.
King, Jonathan, and Michael Bowers. *Gallipoli: Untold
   Stories from War Correspondent Charles Bean and Front-Line
   Anzacs.* Auckland: Random House, 2005.
Perry, Roland. *The Australian Light Horse.* Sydney:
   Hachette Australia, 2009.
Rees, Lucy. *The Horse's Mind.* New York: Arco, 1985.
Stringer, Col. *800 Horsemen.* Queensland, Australia:
   Col Stringer Ministries, 1998.

ARCHIVES

Haydon family archives and personal correspondence,
   Haydon ranch, New South Wales, Australia.
Haydon Horse Stud: www.haydonhorsestud.com.au.